**Bibliographic information published by the German National Library:**

The German National Library lists this publication in the National Bibliography; detailed bibliographic data are available on the Internet at http://dnb.dnb.de .

**Imprint:**

Copyright © 2017 GRIN Verlag, Open Publishing GmbH
Print and binding: Books on Demand GmbH, Norderstedt Germany
ISBN: 9783668605909

**This book at GRIN:**

https://www.grin.com/document/386119

**Ali Mohammad Tarif, Mishkat Nur Rahman, Nazmus Sajid**

# Drones. The future of autonomous delivery?

GRIN Publishing

**GRIN - Your knowledge has value**

Since its foundation in 1998, GRIN has specialized in publishing academic texts by students, college teachers and other academics as e-book and printed book. The website www.grin.com is an ideal platform for presenting term papers, final papers, scientific essays, dissertations and specialist books.

**Visit us on the internet:**

http://www.grin.com/

http://www.facebook.com/grincom

http://www.twitter.com/grin_com

Can Drones Be the Future of Autonomous Delivery

Ali Mohammad Tarif

Mishkat Nur Rahman

Md. Nazmus Sajid

Kulliyyah of Information and Communication Technology (KICT)

International Islamic University Malaysia

# Table of Contents

## Can Drones Be the Future of Autonomous Delivery

Since ancient time, people have faced the necessity to transport goods or merchandizes or mail from one location to another. In almost every part of the world, runners were used by the rulers to convey their messages even before the time it was documented that postal services existed that dates to 255 BC (About history, n.d.). To fulfill their delivery needs, people came up with different solutions such as using animals for delivery purpose and later structured delivery services were introduced. Blake (2010) stated that in the UK, King Henry VII appointed the position "Master of the Posts" and that eventually became the office of the Postmaster General for The Royal Mail back in 1516. But long gone are the days where mediocre technologies or tools were used for delivery purposes. In this modern era, we have many sophisticated delivery services that are using modern day inventions like airplanes, delivery trucks, cargo ships and others. But to take things even further, little mechanical gremlins, drones, is gaining massive popularity to take charge of the delivery system.

Drones are also known as an unmanned aerial vehicle. According to Howell (2015), "In aviation and in space, a drone refers to an unpiloted aircraft or spacecraft" (para. 1). Drones are playing a big part in making deliveries autonomous. By saying autonomous, it is suggested that less human-power needs to be involved in the delivering process and in some cases, it is totally automatic without the need of any human being, all operated by drones and computers.

The traditional way of delivering goods was basically focused on the money that was involved in creating inventories and warehouses. As a result, transports are to travel further distances which increases the fuel consumption. Besides emission of $CO_2$ causes serious damage to our environment. Global warming which endangers our health and jeopardizes our existence is caused because of an excessive amount of $CO_2$ in the air. Kimberly-Clark (as cited in Newing, 2008) stated that if the markets and customers are nearer, then the number of trips to deliver goods will be reduced. This is possible only if the companies share their distributing centers.

The unmanned aerial vehicles or drones have brought a profound change in aerial surveillance and geographical surveying. It can enter an environment that is dangerous for human life. Moreover, for geographical survey and carrying out a confidential operation drones are used in a wide range. For autonomous delivery service, the drone is an emerging idea which can create a massive difference in delivering goods. The autonomous drone can be controlled by the user from the ground by a remote control or onboard controller. They are suitable for delivering goods because of the GPS navigation which will help the customer to track down his or her goods. Smyczyński, Starzec and Granosik (2017) stated that "Operating and navigating outdoors can be very precise due to the availability of GPS signal" (p. 734). Moreover, drones can choose the best route for delivery which saves time and delivers products earlier during emergencies. Therefore, it is strongly agreed that drones really are the future of autonomous delivery as they deliver shipments easily, cost-effective and environmentally friendly.

**Easier Shipment Delivery**

One can deliver goods or emails via couriers or postal delivery services like UK's Royal Mail service, courier services like DHL, UHL uses many different methods to transport the mails or parcels. For local deliveries, traditionally ground vehicles are used to deliver things to the receiver. For international shipping, parcels are sent through airplanes on a cargo ship and when they arrive again the traditional ground vehicle delivery system is used to deliver finally to the actual receiver. In both cases, it is easily understandable that the process is very time-consuming.

Drones can be operated in two ways. One is manual control and the other is automated. For a manually controlled drone, a line of sight of the drone and signal range is very important. According to Andert, Adolf, Goormann, and Dittrich (2011), "Typical missions beyond the line of sight allow only limited manual control due to interrupted and delayed communication with the ground control station" (p. 745). Thus, for delivery drones, an automated system is the only feasible option. In many cases, the drone's flight path from its source to the address of customers is unknown. And since drones fly low, avoiding obstacles is of critical importance. Andert et al. further added that the significance of different usage of UAV or Unmanned Aerial Vehicle at altitude which is low and in places which are completely unknown or known in some parts. For drones to choose the best route, it must be able to identify the route it needs to go and plot the best route or shortest route possible. GPS or Global Positioning System, in this case, solves the problem of finding optimal route for drone navigation. Peng, Lin, and Dai (2016) stated that "Similar to setting up the GPS navigation before we drive, the UAV navigation system will generate an optimal or shortest path." (p. 984). Moreover, it also needs to know how to avoid human-made and nonhuman-made obstacles if those are on its flight path. Many techniques and sensors can be applied to resolve the issue. Peng et al. further argued that using lightweight and cheap digital cameras, vision-based algorithms can be implemented on drones for them to be able to avoid obstacles. Thus, drones can choose the optimal flight route to deliver goods to its customers, making delivery of shipments easier.

Natural disasters are a common phenomenon of nature. Every year many parts of the world are hit by disasters like hurricanes, floods, earthquakes and so on. Since drones are an aerial vehicle, they can provide support to rescue teams after natural disaster faster than ground-based operations for immediate and emergency help. According to Hutson (2017), there is a lot of evidence that shows "…drones may have certain advantages over traditional search-and-rescue efforts — including speed" (para. 3). In Africa, delivery drones are acting as a life saver. Peters (2017) stated how autonomous drone saved the life of pregnant women. The mother was about to die. The drone delivered seven units of red blood cells, four units of plasma and two units of plasma, which was more than what she required. We can also find some Islamic perspective here. From the Holy Al-Quran, Surah 5, Verse 32, we get to know that, "If anyone saves a life, it shall be as though he had saved the lives of all mankind". From the verse, we can understand how important it is to help others and the significance of saving human lives. And in the above mentioned life-threatening scenario, the use of drone saved the woman's life.

In short, we think the drone can become the next big thing in delivery service. Amazon, the world's biggest electronic commerce and cloud computing company has acknowledged the futuristic concept of autonomous drones for delivering goods.

**Cost Efficiency**

Operating cost plays a big factor in any company or organization. And for logistic companies or goods or products delivery companies, this cost has a drastic impact. Every company wants to be more efficient. They want the service operation cost lower than the amount they earn. The bigger the difference, the better the profit. For many logistic companies, this is a very big concern. Multi-billion-dollar companies like UPS, FedEx, DHL, Amazon want to reduce the delivery cost without compromising the quality of service. Hence, drones come into play. Kim (2016) stated that Deutsche Bank speculated that using drones and mechanical robots to automatically deliver products, would have been Amazon, Inc's most prominent price lessening policy. Kim further added that the Deutsche Bank explained the matter further by showing price samples of a typical delivery cost, in which, it was shown that Amazon would have charged far less than other shipping or logistic or product delivery companies. It clearly portrays the idea that using drones is very cost efficient.

Drones are generally compact in size compared to any ground vehicle and it has lesser mechanical parts than those ground vehicles have. The maintenance of drones is easier and operation cost is lower. Lee (2017) suggested that "It is also possible to reduce the cost of maintenance in a drone delivery system since drones are less expensive than ground vehicles and easier to repair" (p. 1). Using gasoline to power ground vehicles is significantly costly since fossil fuel such as diesel or petrol costs more. Using electricity, on the other hand, is proving to be cheaper. According to Yamauchi (n.d.), people who are using electricity powered vehicle, on average, saves about $60US every month just for not using gasoline. So, we can understand that using electricity rather than gasoline will cut fuel consumption cost, thus making it cheaper and efficient. Drones are generally powered by batteries. And these batteries are charged up by using electrical power. And it gives drones their working capability. Since drones are much lighter than ground vehicles, they consume less electrical energy than their ground electrical vehicle counterparts. Ferrandez, Harbison, Weber, Sturges, and Rich (2016) in their study found the following:

> Conversely, the energy efficiencies achieved with a drone far surpassed that of the truck when simulated deliveries to one hundred customers over a 100 km square distance of delivery. This is likely due to the fact that a drone is far more efficient due to less overall

vehicle weight, less heat loss, and less friction even though the drone is required to traverse nearly twice the distance. (p. 388)

Moreover, scientific advancement in the field of batteries made them more efficient over older battery technology. Moore and Schneider (2001, as cited in Lee, 2017) argued that batteries that are based on lithium-ion technology coupled with high energy density are more efficient to increase flight time of drones rather than batteries using nickel-cadmium and nickel metal hybrid batteries. And with the inception of modularly based drones, the performance is further increased by changing batteries automatically, instead of wasting time to recharge the drone's battery. More working time equals more efficiency in the delivery system. Lee (2017) further claimed that:

> A modular design with swappable batteries is expected to perform better than drones with integrated batteries in terms of readiness. Furthermore, since a set of drone types with distinct capabilities is necessary to accomplish various types of delivery tasks, modularity can reduce the overall fleet size thanks to module sharing. (p. 1)

If the drone fleet size is small, the operation cost will also be low, and so will be energy consumption. And all these translate to one thing: drones being cost-efficient.

Drones that are used for the delivery system are almost fully automated. Shenoy and Keshavan (2017) have claimed that, as communication technology is advancing, the need for human connection has lessened to have a system that works fully automatically. So, delivery companies might not need extra manpower to run their delivery operation smoothly. And fewer people involvement means less cost. Thus, the company now doesn't need to pay extra to those people. Drones, therefore, are the excellent choice for delivery companies to reduce their operating cost also.

To conclude, drones have excellent cost efficiency for any delivery company as they provide the company with options to save fuel cost, operation cost and reduces manual labor cost.

**Environmentally friendly**

UAV/Drone technology has allowed groundbreaking opportunities in preserving the environment and increasing the yield of crops. In modern time people are continuously trying to preserve the environment like cars are using electricity as an alternative to fossil fuel, usage of solar energy has become common for domestic uses and industrial places. Similarly, autonomous drones can play a tremendous role in increasing agricultural production and reduce emission of carbon dioxide.

Drones can be used for crop identification, crop acreage estimation, crop condition assessment and stress detection. Besides, it can also be used to estimate and model crop yield, soil mapping, to monitor and manage irrigation. Drones are programmed with remote sensing technology to carry out these jobs. Hafsal (2016) stated that drones can make precision agriculture more sustainable. Autonomous drones have the ability to do things which a farmer cannot. It can spray acres of lands with insecticides within a day that might take a farmer about 15-16 days. Thus, it is helping them to maximize income and returns on investment in the end. Using normalized difference vegetation method index a mapping method drones can easily detect green vegetation zones. Earlier this surveillance was performed by satellite or plane but with the drone, it has become cost-effective, so early warning of crop stress and crop health issues can be provided within centimeters. For supervising agricultural system, drones provide scientific images which pave the way to operate irrigation properly. It provides valuable information through which farmers can quantify the precise amount of water needed to be applied in different parts of the land rather than pouring at the same rate. Again, most of the crops can be severely damaged by diseases before any visible signs like de-colorization of leaves. These are not sometimes visible to our naked eyes, but drones with their multispectral cameras which uses special filters to detect early stages of diseases. With the collected data farmers can tell where to spray before the disease can infect crops. As the world population is increasing rapidly, so declination of crop yield can seriously affect the food supply for this growing population.

Carbon dioxide is one of the greenhouse gases that are emitted to the environment due to several natural processes and human activities. It is basically created due to the burning of fossil fuels (oil, natural gas, coal), trees and wood products. With the advancement of human civilization, the amount of carbon dioxide emission to the atmosphere has steadily increased, trapping that heat and warming the planetary surface. As a result, the icebergs are melting down and causing the sea level to rise. Carbon dioxide is not only affecting the atmosphere, it is also making the ocean and affecting different sea organisms. So, Carbon dioxide emissions must be controlled to preserve the environment. Drones emit less amount of carbon dioxide compared to ground vehicles like trucks, vans or cargos. When the delivery range of a package is not very far, then drone can be counted as an option. Drones run by fossil fuel powered electricity which can emit a large amount of carbon dioxide if parcels are heavy. They are suitable when the number of recipients is significantly large in a small landscape. Moreover, unmanned aerial vehicles (UAV) are offering new ways to manage climate changes. Earlier scientists used to measure albedo via satellite or sensors, but they cannot be moved to take the albedo of nearby locations. But with drones, they can take measurements of wherever place they needed. As a result, they can calculate which portion of the earth's surface is radiating more amount of solar energy. According to Opfer (2017), drones are really cost effective when it comes to capturing footage of large area of land. Like during deforestation or volcanic eruption, it's really expensive and risky to send a helicopter or plane to the spot but drones can easily sweep footage of those vulnerable areas.

In short, autonomous drones can preserve our environment by emitting less amount of carbon dioxide to the atmosphere. It can be the future because it has lessened the human effort with maximum accuracy.

In conclusion, we would like to say that with the rapid development of e-commerce, customers are prioritizing on the variety and the perceived quality of the delivery service. As a result, vendors are trying to provide their customers with the best delivery experiences by improving delivery times. Customers prefer quickness in delivery, despite costing more than the traditional way by ground vehicles. We can see how people pay for premiums to receive items in a single day. Delivering through drones can also be really cost effective as Smyczyński, Starzec and Granosik (2017) stated that "Operating and navigating outdoors can be very precise due to the availability of GPS signal" (p. 734). So, autonomous drones choose the best route with help of GPS to deliver goods whereas ground vehicles face various obstacles and consume both times and increase cost. That is why it is strongly believed that drones are the future of autonomous delivery because it is easy to deliver shipments, cost-efficient and moreover it's environment-friendly

Now, it is suggested to revolutionize the way of delivering things by engaging autonomous drone in delivery infrastructure. This can be done by replacing ground vehicles to some extent with drones. As we mentioned before that autonomous drones are environmentally friendly due to less emission of carbon as it can fly very far to its destination or when a delivery route has fewer recipients. A battery-powered drone will surely show tremendous results when it comes to cost efficiency and emissions. Moreover, drones can minimize the rate of errors when it comes to delivering products to humans. Besides people must undergo different pieces of training and workshops before achieving expertise on something. But well programmed autonomous drones are more sensible and error-free while providing delivery services.

Another important thing that should address in this paper is the use of autonomous drones to gain more accuracy. Drones are conducting operations safely and extracting pinpoint data from those vulnerable areas which are beyond human reach. They are playing a tremendous role while it comes to delivering medic kit in disastrous areas. Opfer (2017) explained how researchers are using drones to calculate the temperature, ash height and spewing of sulfur dioxide from an erupting volcano despite satellite footages. Again, to determine the causes of melting glaciers in the Arctic, to study the underwater wildlife and how they are adapting to this continuous climate changes are now discoverable because of the multidimensional footages captured by autonomous drones. Likewise, drones are being worked efficient and productive in the agricultural sector. It has revolutionized the concept of farming by precise agriculture which will play a vital role in the future. For analyzing soil and field, planting seeds, spraying insecticides, crop monitoring and to assess crop health automated drones are being the first priority for the farmers.

The future of global industries will be shaped by autonomous drones, thus saving them time, costs, energy and wastage of resources and manpower. With 3D printing technology attached with drone's, constructors can maintain and repair damaged infrastructure. Autonomous drones can have a tremendous impact on mass surveillance by identifying potential threats and immediately transmitting it to response team. So, to sum up we would like to say that the biggest reasons why drones are being adopted worldwide are because it requires less effort, time and energy. And this is the same reason why autonomous drones are the futuristic way of delivery service.

# References

*About history.* (n.d.). Retrieved from the Universal Postal Union: http://www.upu.int/en/the-upu/history/about-history.html

Andert, F., Adolf, F., Goormann, L., & Dittrich, J. (2011). Mapping and path planning in complex environments: An obstacle avoidance approach for an unmanned helicopter. *2011 IEEE International Conference on Robotics and Automation* (pp. 745-750). Shanghai: IEEE. doi:10.1109/ICRA.2011.5979535

Blake, H. (2010, June 10). *The Royal Mail: a history of the British postal service.* Retrieved from The Telegraph: http://www.telegraph.co.uk/news/uknews/royal-mail/7814591/The-Royal-Mail-a-history-of-the-British-postal-service.html

Fernandez, S. M., Harbison, T., Weber, T., Sturges, R., & Rich, R. (2016). Optimization of a truck-drone in a tandem delivery network using k-means and genetic algorithm. *Journal of Industrial Engineering and Management, 9*(2), 374-388. doi:http://dx.doi.org/10.3926/jiem.1929

Hafsal, L. P. (2016). *Precision Agriculture with Unmanned Aerial Vehicles for SMC estimations - Towards a More Sustainable Agriculture.* Elverum. Retrieved from https://brage.bibsys.no/xmlui/bitstream/handle/11250/2394352/Hafsal.pdf?sequence=1

Howell, E. (2015, June 2). *What Is A Drone?* Retrieved from SPACE.com: https://www.space.com/29544-what-is-a-drone.html

Hutson, M. (2017, September 10). *Hurricanes Show Why Drones Are the Future of Disaster Relief.* Retrieved from MACH: https://www.nbcnews.com/mach/science/hurricanes-show-why-drones-are-future-disaster-relief-ncna799961

Kim, E. (2016, June 15). *The most staggering part of Amazon's upcoming drone delivery service.* Retrieved from Business Insider: http://www.businessinsider.com/cost-savings-from-amazon-drone-deliveries-2016-6/?IR=T

Lee, J. (2017). Optimization of a modular drone delivery system. *2017 Annual IEEE International Systems Conference (SysCon)* (pp. 1-8). Montreal, QC: IEEE. doi:10.1109/SYSCON.2017.7934790

Newing, R. (2008, October 8). *Transport: Finding better ways to deliver the goods.* Retrieved
from Financial Times: https://www.ft.com/content/07566cb8-9400-11dd-b277-
0000779fd18c

Opfer, C. (2017). *What are eco-drones?* Retrieved from HowStuffWorks:
https://science.howstuffworks.com/environmental/green-tech/sustainable/eco-drones.htm

Peng, X.-Z., Lin, H.-Y., & Dai, J.-M. (2016). Path Planning and Obstacle Avoidance for Vision
Guided Quadrotor. *2016 12th IEEE International Conference on Control and Automation
(ICCA)* (pp. 984-989). Kathmandu: IEEE. doi:10.1109/ICCA.2016.7505408

Peters, A. (2017, August 24). *Filled With Blood And Drugs, These Delivery Drones Are Saving
Lives In Africa.* Retrieved from Fast Company:
https://www.fastcompany.com/40457183/filled-with-blood-and-medical-supplies-these-
delivery-drones-are-saving-lives-in-africa

Shenoy, R., & Keshavan, B. (2017). Hybrid drone for data transaction. *2017 IEEE International
Conference on Smart Energy Grid Engineering (SAGE)* (pp. 238-241). Oshawa, ON:
IEEE. doi:10.1109/SEGE.2017.8052805

Smyczyński, P., Starzec, Ł., & Granosik, G. (2017). Autonomous drone control system for object
tracking: Flexible system design with implementation example. *2017 22nd International
Conference on Methods and Models in Automation and Robotics (MMAR)* (pp. 734-738).
Miedzyzdroje: IEEE. doi:10.1109/MMAR.2017.8046919

Yamauchi, M. (n.d.). *DRIVING ON ELECTRICITY IS CHEAPER THAN GAS IN ALL 50
STATES.* Retrieved from Plugless: https://www.pluglesspower.com/learn/driving-
electricity-cheaper-gas-50-states/

# YOUR KNOWLEDGE HAS VALUE

- We will publish your bachelor's and master's thesis, essays and papers

- Your own eBook and book - sold worldwide in all relevant shops

- Earn money with each sale

Upload your text at www.GRIN.com and publish for free

www.ingramcontent.com/pod-product-compliance
Lightning Source LLC
LaVergne TN
LVHW080120070326
832902LV00015B/2686